HILLS & M

RICHARD TAYLOR

COLLINS & BROWN

First published in Great Britain in 2003
by Collins & Brown Limited
64 Brewery Road
London N7 9NT

A member of **Chrysalis** Books plc

Distributed in the United States and Canada by Sterling Publishing Co.,
387 Park Avenue South, New York, NY 10016 USA

1 3 5 7 9 8 6 4 2

British Library Cataloguing-in-Publication Data:
A catalogue record for this book is available from the British Library.

ISBN 1-85585-816-9

Editorial Director: Roger Bristow
Project managed by Emma Baxter
Copy-edited by Katie Hardwicke
Designed by Alison Shackleton
Photographed by Ben Wray

Printed and bound in China

CONTENTS

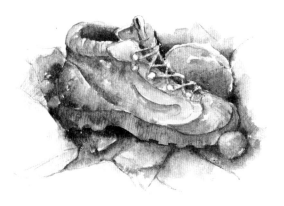

Tools and Materials

Because this book is intended mainly as a 'field guide' that you can take with you on painting expeditions in the hills and mountains, this chapter looks at some of the tools and materials that I find most useful to carry with me when working outdoors.

Start by choosing your paper. Sketchpads are the most useful – in particular those that are ringbound, as they give a hardbacked surface on which to work. These sketchpads come in a wide range of types and sizes – I prefer a 210 x 297 mm (8¼ x 11¾ in) or 297 x 420 mm (11¾ x 16½ in) pad of at least 300 gsm weight watercolour paper. This allows me to use a lot of water in the knowledge that the paper will stay reasonably flat and not 'cockle'.

I also carry a small pocket-size drawing pad for making quick pencil sketches and notes of the linear and tonal structures of my subjects before I start the finished picture.

Watercolour and Pencil (opposite)
The translucent qualities of watercolour paints allow them to work particularly well with pencil – not just as guidelines. You can also enhance a watercolour painting by drawing a few well chosen lines on top of a dry wash.

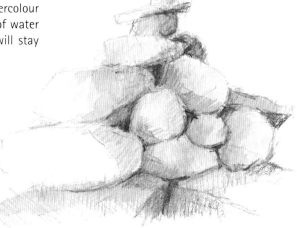

Watercolour Pencil Study
You can utilize the water-soluble and the graphic/linear qualities of water-soluble pencils particularly well when sketching rocks and boulders. Building up a series of tones becomes great fun using these highly portable materials.

Pads and Sketchbooks
Watercolour and cartridge-paper pads are essential for outdoor use, because they are compact and allow you to keep all of your work flat and held together. They can be used for visual notes to remind you of the scene, and personal thoughts, as well as for more 'finished' paintings (which are rarely completed on-site).

Travelling Light

A few selected pencils are a valuable asset to your sketching kit – carrying too many only complicates matters, as you have to think about which ones to use. Graphite pencils come in a variety of grades. Artists usually make use of the B (soft) grade pencils: 6B is the softest and gives rich, dark tones, while B is the lightest and offers a subtle range of greys.

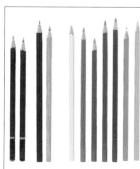

B

2B

4B

6B

USING THE PAPER

Watercolour can be particularly effective in producing sharp highlights – leave a flash of the white paper showing through the initial wash to allow your paintings to 'sparkle'.

Sketching pencils are very soft graphite pencils with thick leads, and are good for making quick, bold sketches. They are readily available and come in a wide range of grades – B is the hardest grade used by most artists, and 6B the softest for practical use.

Water-soluble pencils make a normal graphite mark, but have an additional quality – the mark can be washed over with water to produce a soft, watercolour-type grey tone. Water-soluble pencils are available in different grades, although these are usually limited to soft, medium and hard.

There are many advantages of tonal sketching. First, try squinting by half-closing your eyes – you will see a simplified, tonal version of your subject. By recording these tones you will see where the dark, medium and light areas of your composition are before you begin to paint. Second, you can draw or make a sketch on any type of paper – you can even use water-soluble pencils effectively on drawing paper. Third, sketching materials are easily portable – you can slip a pencil and a small pad into your pocket wherever you go.

When drawing and sketching, practise your techniques – hold your pencil in two different ways. To sketch a quick outline, hold your pencil as you would if you were writing, and draw with the tip. However, when you want to shade or block in an area, you will need to change you grip. Place your finger along the length of the pencil so that you draw with the edge of the lead. Each style of drawing serves a very different purpose, and it is well worth practising to master each style.

Sketching in monochrome can often be a very useful method of assessing and analysing the tonal values of your subject without getting too concerned with colour at an early stage. Various tools can be used for drawing in monochrome: graphite sketching pencils are the most useful to carry in your sketching kit. These can be divided into two categories – standard drawing pencils and water-soluble pencils.

Sometimes it is a good idea to make a few 'visual notes' using coloured pencils to capture the nature of your subject – the colour, shape and structure, for example – especially when you are short of time, or in an inhospitable environment.

Standard coloured pencils are highly effective for sketches. They are available in a large range of colours but I strongly recommend that you limit yourself to seven: deep green, sap green, olive green, yellow, raw sienna, burnt umber and ultramarine.

Water-soluble colour pencils are much softer than standard coloured pencils as they are solidified sticks of watercolour pigment. They create highly-textured marks when used on watercolour paper. They are, however, most effective when water is washed over them, turning the pigment into watercolour paint. You can also dip them into water and use them to draw directly onto painted areas, darkening such sections as you choose – again, this is something that you will need to practise

PAINTS AND BRUSHES
Watercolour tins come in a variety of styles. I prefer no more than 12 pans – these colours are included in most sets, but you can buy replacements to create your own personal palette. Some tins include a brush, but you may prefer to carry a selection of you own preferred brushes.

You can use palette lids for mixing colours.

Synthetic brushes are the best type to take out on painting expeditions. Modern ones are close in quality to natural-hair brushes.

It is a good idea to carry a small plastic water dipper in your bag, rather than taking bottles of water – you will rarely need that much to paint with. Dippers can be purchased singly from art-supply stores, or sometimes are included as part of a watercolour tin or set.

and experiment with to discover the method of working that suits you best.

A small watercolour tin that holds pan paints fits easily into a pocket, and I can change the colour pans to suit the mood of the day and the subject matter. These tins often come with a retractable brush, and more elaborate models sometimes have a small water container built-in as well. I keep my selection of brushes simple – I use one large wash brush, one medium and one small detail brush (all round-headed), plus one flat-headed or chisel brush. For outdoor expeditions I use synthetic brushes as these are a perfectly acceptable alternative to animal-hair brushes, and are considerably cheaper to replace when lost. However, I do use natural sable brushes when working in the studio. All of my outdoor painting items are kept in a strong canvas backpack that can withstand rough treatment in hilly or mountainous environments.

WATER-SOLUBLE GRAPHITE PENCIL STUDY
The harshness of cliff and rock faces are complemented by the cold, slate grey tone created by water-soluble graphite pencils. These combine the tonal qualities of 4B–6B pencils with the softness of watercolour washes.

TECHNIQUES

Recording the immense vistas to be found amongst hilly or mountainous landscapes is always a challenge for any artist. It is, therefore, highly advisable to become familiar with a few practical techniques to help you make the most of your painting time surrounded by such breathtaking views. As always, practise will soon help you to develop all the skills you need to paint in such an environment.

GRADUATED WASH

The one thing that you can't help but notice when standing in open, rolling countryside is that the hills in the far distance will usually appear to be lighter in tone than those closer to you in the immediate foreground. To help to record this sense of space and distance, you can apply a graduated wash across the landscape and, when this has dried, identify the physical features of the landscape by painting onto the established 'underpainting'.

The first part of the graduated wash involves applying water to the entire 'ground' area with a large brush. Before this

---

CREATING A GRADUATED WASH

1 Lightly dampen the paper with clean water. From the top of the paper, wash raw sienna down towards the centre using a smooth, unhurried side-to-side motion.

2 Next, from the base of the paper, apply sap green and a touch of raw sienna and wash this upwards using the same motion as with raw sienna. When the two colours meet, allow them to mix naturally.

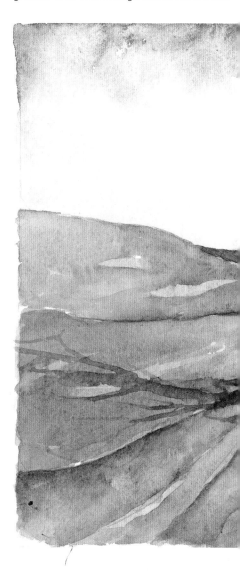

has time to dry, apply a watery wash of raw sienna and, using side-to-side brushstrokes, pull the paint down towards the base of the composition. Then, quickly, create a mixture of sap green with a hint of raw sienna (this prevents the colour mix from looking too unnatural) and reverse the process. Apply the green paint to the base of the paper and pull the paint upwards, still using side-to-side brushstrokes. This will blend with the raw sienna underwash, creating a covering of paint that goes from light on the horizon to dark in the immediate foreground without any obvious break.

DISTANT HILLS
This spring scene was alive with the movement of shadows cast by clouds scudding across the cool sky. The muted tones of the distant hills change subtlely towards the foreground.

USING DIFFERENT BRUSHES

Understanding and learning to use colours is very important for painters but it is equally important to understand the implements used for applying these colours to paper – brushes.

There are many types of brushes available in art stores, and they all have their uses, but a simple choice of just three or four brushes will be all that you could ever need for painting out of doors in 'out of the way' places.

The most important thing to remember is that different brushes make different marks - this is the key choice that you need to make: do you choose a large brush which will hold a lot of water and deposit this in a swathe of paint that will run and bleed onto wet paper, or do you choose a small brush that will make marks similar to thick pencil lines? Both have a valuable role to play in the painting process - but when to choose each brush?

Usually, your choice of a large brush will be for laying a background wash where little detail is required - a large brush helps you to complete this quickly without any fussy brushstrokes.

A smaller brush will be used more frequently in the foreground where the detail will be sharper and cracks in rocks, and the individual shapes of pebbles and stones can be suggested with much more control over the flow of paint.

DIFFERENT BRUSHES

1 *A large brush will effortlessly cover a large area of paper, leaving no evidence or suggestion of brush marks.*

2 *A small brush will create a very different finish. As they hold less paint they have to be reloaded frequently. These are best for 'drawing' fine details.*

ROCK FACE
The sheer scale of these rock faces was intimidating at first but it is easy to become totally absorbed in the painting process and to forget such things. A large brush was used for the solid rock and a smaller brush for the detailed cracks and fissures.

FOOTHILLS

The far distant sight of violet tinged, softly rolling hills is one that invariably makes artists want to reach for their watercolour tins. The soft greens of these gentle terrains combined with the natural siennas are a pleasure to paint in any season, and in most weather conditions – torrential rain, of course, excepted!

TONE AND DISTANCE

The effect of distance, evident in all panoramic landscapes, is best created by the use of tone – that is making colours lighter in parts and darker in other areas.

Sometimes it can be helpful to practise creating tones by using just one colour (monochrome) or even with a grey toned water-soluble graphite pencil, looking to ensure that the tone always increases from a light distant background to a considerably darker foreground.

When you feel that you are happy with creating tones with single colours, then try mixing some colours, such as the violets that often appear to cloak distant hills, and again, create as many different tones as you can. This can be done either by changing the balance of the paint mixture to darken the tone, or by diluting with more water to lighten it, creating a tint.

CHANGING TONES
The effect of distance is conveyed in this painting by lightening the tone of the overlapping hills as they recede.

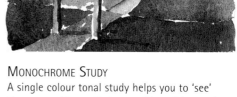

PENCIL STUDY
Water-soluble graphite pencils are highly portable and excellent for making quick preliminary sketches.

MONOCHROME STUDY
A single colour tonal study helps you to 'see' the range of tones that you will need to create in a composition.

ULTRAMARINE

ALIZARIN
CRIMSON

CERULEAN
BLUE

ALIZARIN
CRIMSON

The linear qualities of the old trail, vanishing into a range of soft violet hills, illustrates the way that a sense of perspective can be created on a flat surface.

CERULEAN BLUE   ULTRAMARINE

ADDING WATER

Experiment with single colours at first - how much water can you add until you lose the colour completely?

MIXING COLOURS

Now try mixing colours. This introduces a new element. How much of each colour do you need to mix to alter the tone?

TONAL MIXING

The variety of green tones required to paint a well-lit hillside landscape can be extensive – for this reason it is a good idea to practise using a manufactured green and altering the tone to both light and dark. Sap green is a particularly good colour for this type of exercise. On its own it is not a particularly 'natural' green, but this can be altered easily without losing the clarity of the colour. Add cadmium yellow to the sap green to produce a lighter green, seeing how far you can take the tone (by adding water) before it becomes almost invisible. Then, work in the other direction. Add ultramarine to sap green and see how dark you can make the colour whilst still maintaining a hint of green.

Once you can do this, you will be more than ready to paint grass covered hills in any lighting conditions.

ULTRAMARINE

SAP GREEN

CADMIUM YELLOW

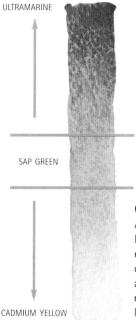

GREEN TONES
Adding darker and lighter colours to an existing 'medium' colour can provide a wealth of different tones for use in landscapes.

Dark tones can be used when painting hills to help define specific shapes. A shadow painted 'behind' a small hillock will usually push it forward into the middle ground or foreground.

Highlights in the landscape, often seen when directional sunlight is hitting patches of ground, are best created by the addition of yellow to the grass mixture.

HIGHLIGHTS

The contrast between the highlights on the tops of the hills and the shadows in the valley made this particular scene very appealing to paint.

SHADOWS

Watching clouds roll over the far horizon, casting shadows across the open hillside, is a wondrous sight to observe. It can, however, complicate the issue for painters. Suddenly, you find that you need a much wider range of greens to cope with the transient effects of the weather.

It's time now to practise extending the potential of sap green, cadmium yellow and ultramarine by the addition of burnt umber – try as many combinations as possible and compare these with greens created by mixing your own greens from blues and yellows.

Also, you will find that introducing olive green into the far distant hills (mixed with a touch of raw sienna) at the graduated wash stage will increase the tonal variety. Paint with as many of these greens as you can when establishing the basic green of the hills. When this has dried, mix the darkest and use a small brush to 'draw' the shadows onto the green paint surface.

CHANGING LIGHT
The way that the light fell onto these rolling hills, changing tone and thrusting flashes of highlight forward, required an instant response to the scene.

SAP GREEN   ULTRAMARINE

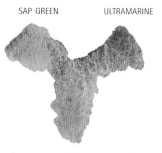

SAP GREEN   CADMIUM YELLOW

SAP GREEN   ULTRAMARINE   BURNT
                              UMBER

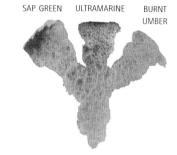

ALTERING A PROPRIETARY GREEN
Cleaner and fresher greens can be created by using a proprietary green as a base and adding yellows, blues and browns to alter its values.

The hills in the distance need to be applied freely with a large brush - they should also contain an element of blue or violet to ensure that they 'sink' into the background.

The foreground greens need to 'sparkle' a little to suggest a sharper focus - even dark greens can be bright. This is achieved by not mixing muddying browns in with them.

OLIVE GREEN

SAP GREEN

ULTRAMARINE   CADMIUM YELLOW   ULTRAMARINE   RAW SIENNA

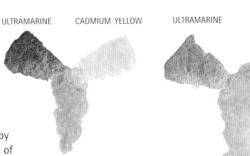

MIXING GREENS

Try creating your own greens by mixing different combinations of blue and yellow – they will often turn out to be 'muddy' colours.

BACKPACK STUDY

Having come this far along the trail, through the foothills and lush meadows, it is perfectly acceptable to sit down and take a break. This could, however, be seen as a waste of painting time!

Instead you could take a few moments to make a sketch or two and why not turn to your equipment?

Most modern backpacks are designed with personal safety in mind and are, therefore, usually very bright colours, creating a marked contrast with the olive greens and soft violets of the landscape.

Cadmium orange is a good colour to use as a base, adding cadmium yellow to create the lighter patches, and using ultramarine and alizarin crimson for the shaded areas. Subjects like this are best painted onto dry paper – this allows you to achieve some broken brushstrokes as the paint drags across the textured watercolour paper surface, allowing highlights to develop naturally, adding a slightly old and 'well worn' appearance to the backpack.

Most mountaineering or trail-walking equipment today is designed to be spotted from a long distance – cadmium orange was the ideal colour for this backpack.

QUICK STUDY
The slightly battered and faded look of this well-used backpack added to its 'character' and ultimate appeal as a subject for a quick sketchbook study.

The edges of the rucksack were highlighted by leaving them unpainted, allowing flashes of white paper to show through.

A purple colour mixed from ultramarine and alizarin crimson was applied to the damp cadmium orange underwash to create the shadow colours here.

ROCKS

Sooner or later, you will leave the soft green foothills behind and encounter rocks and boulders. This is a much harsher environment where the soft shapes and tones of the hills give way to hard cracks and fissures. These require not just different colours, but different brushes and a whole new, sharper way of painting.

ROCK FACES

The very nature of rocks and crags means that you do not have to concentrate quite so much on colour – more on form, shape and suggested detail.

To paint a group of rock faces, start by loosely pulling a wet brush loaded with raw sienna across dry paper, covering the entire rocky area. The result will be an uneven covering of paint with several white flashes of paper showing where the brush has not fully covered the paper. These flashes will act as highlights along the rock edges.

FLAT-HEADED BRUSHES

1 A large, chisel-headed brush will create a very broad sweep of paint, with excellent covering power.

2 Use a small chisel-headed brush on its side to produce much sharper, linear marks which are particularly suited to sharp rock faces.

Next, mix a dark, stone-coloured wash using raw umber, burnt sienna and ultramarine and quickly wash this onto the shaded or darkest areas of rock that you can see. As long as the underwash is still slightly damp this will dry with soft edges.

When this has fully dried, you can start to paint the sharp shadows underneath the rocks and in between the cracks and fissures with a darker mix, using the tip of a small brush to obtain really sharp foreground definitions.

STREWN BOULDERS
Whilst a collection of so many rocks and boulders may initially appear off-putting, the painting method is not so difficult as it might seem – the key is to make the underwash work for you to 'suggest' the different textures.

The tops of flat rocks are best created by simply leaving the underwash to show through and creating the three-dimensional effect by painting the sides of the rock.

Cracks are best created by 'drawing' onto dry paper with the edge of a chisel-headed brush, or the point of a small brush, using a colour mixture of burnt umber and ultramarine.

STEPPING STONES

The main feature of these stepping stones is the way in which water has been used to create a wealth of wet-looking textures.

By applying clean water to drying paint you can achieve this effect – the water pushes the paint outwards, breaking up its regular drying pattern, scattering the particles of paint. As they dry, so the 'watermark' can be seen, providing an appearance of wetness and texture. This is a particularly appropriate technique to use when painting stepping stones, or any rocks and boulders in or on the edge of rivers.

RAW UMBER   BURNT UMBER   ULTRAMARINE

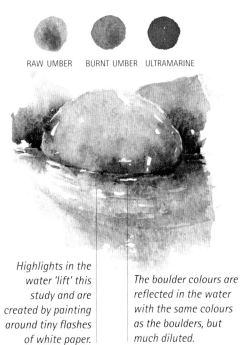

Highlights in the water 'lift' this study and are created by painting around tiny flashes of white paper.

The boulder colours are reflected in the water with the same colours as the boulders, but much diluted.

REFLECTIONS
Observe how the shadows at the base of this boulder follow the gradual curve of the rock – work onto damp paper to help create this smoothness in your painting.

FAST-FLOWING WATER
Highlights and shadows are more predictable on these rounded rocks than on harsher rock faces. Watermarks – created when wet paint is applied onto dry paint – suggest texture.

The texture on boulders such as these is best obtained by applying the appropriate colour and, just as the paint is beginning to dry, drop some pure water from a small brush onto the paint – this creates a textured effect as it dries.

Rocks and boulders do contain colour - always look carefully for the green algae tinge, or the mineral veins which are best painted with burnt sienna.

The key to painting moving water is to leave as much white paper as you dare, using only the paint from the rocks to create coloured reflections.

Hiking Boot Study

After scrambling over rocks, the relief of removing hiking boots is unparalleled – and a wonderful opportunity for a quick sketch.

The very nature of this particular subject will offer a slightly different approach from usual. First, apply a raw sienna underwash to dry paper and quickly wash in the darkest areas using burnt umber with just a touch of ultramarine.

When this is dry you may find it helpful to recreate the details – laces, eyelets, ribbed soles – by drawing onto the watercolour with a water-soluble pencil. This gives a sharp linear quality to the study, yet still allows you the option of softening any of the lines with a plain water wash at any time.

Once you are happy with the boot, create a very strong mixture of burnt umber and ultramarine and paint this directly underneath the sole using a small brush to create the shadows which will visually anchor the boot to the ground.

The curves on this boot were created by allowing the underwash to show, complemented by a few flashes of white paper to suggest highlights next to creases.

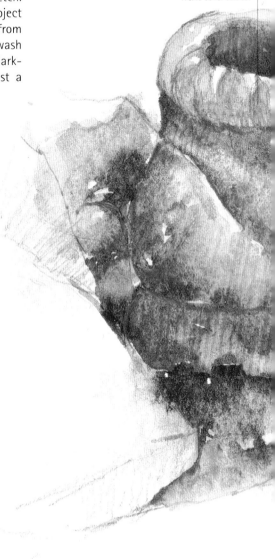

Using Water-soluble Pencil

This old boot was almost camouflaged, positioned between sandy coloured rocks and stones. This forced the addition of a new set of marks – pencil – to really make sure that it stood out from the background watercolour wash.

Laces were suggested by both painting and drawing behind them, creating a set of intertwining 'negative' shapes which were visually pushed forward by darkening the tones behind.

Due to the ribbed nature of this old boot, a water-soluble graphite pencil was used to draw detail onto a dry watercolour wash.

HUTS AND SHELTERS

Anyone who has ventured into the higher hills during the winter season will know how welcoming the sight of a solid mountain shelter can be. But these are not the only kinds of shelter to be found in the landscape – tents and wooden cabins each serve different purposes, but are just as valuable when the weather turns bad or night begins to fall.

TENTS

Having put up your tent and cooked a meal in wild, remote country, there is often little to do as dusk encroaches but paint the scene in which you find yourself.

The colour of modern tents always makes them stand out clearly from the backdrop, whatever the weather conditions. The key elements to consider when painting tents is the tautness of the canvas and the sharp edges that these create – all of these are best painted onto dry paper, using a small brush to almost 'draw' the tight creases onto a highly coloured base. This also applies to ropes – use a suggestion of a few key supports only, as over fussy detail can detract from the central image.

CADMIUM YELLOW	CADMIUM RED	ULTRAMARINE	ALIZARIN CRIMSON

The edges of the taut canvas are best left as plain white paper – a very thin sliver will work well.

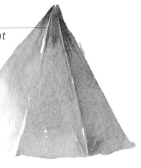

TAUT CANVAS
The way in which ropes and pegs exert pressure on the bottoms and tops of tents creates the tautness and tension of the canvas – these sections are worthy of special attention before embarking on a full-scale painting.

TWILIGHT TONES
The soft violet tones forming in the dusk sky settled gently across the landscape and the tent, producing an irresistible subject, awash with colour and contrasts.

Canvas tents can hold a wide range of tones. The highlights – either faded canvas or where the light is catching – can be created by blotting the damp paint during the drying process.

The taut nature of stretched canvas is a key feature of tents. This is best recorded with smooth brushstrokes and hard edges at the point where the canvas is tightest.

Stone Mountain Shelter

Stone is a universal building material, often found in mountainous areas where it is quarried from the rock faces.

The very nature of the system for obtaining rocks means that the individual stones will be of different shapes and sizes – this is part of the appeal to the artist as a stone wall can often appear like a complex pattern full of light and dark tones.

I find that the best way to paint stone walls is to apply a watery wash of raw umber and encourage this to dry unevenly by dropping water onto the paint as it dries. This will disturb the gum arabic binder and disperse the pigment in the paint. When this irregular colour wash has dried, I use a small brush to almost 'draw' in between the shapes of some of the rocks with burnt umber. I then wash some of this colour into the surrounding stones to avoid lots of hard edges. When this is dry, I sometimes sharpen a few selected lines with a dark mixture of burnt umber and ultramarine.

First, apply a watery underwash with a medium brush.

Sharpen a few lines around the stones once the paper is dry – this will avoid 'bleeds'.

Establish the colour of the stone by dropping paint onto the underwash while it is still damp.

Corner stones are often the biggest to be found in a building. Try to paint one side of the corner stone a little darker than the other to create a three dimensional effect.

Stone Wall
Allow the dark stone colour to run down onto the grass or ground colour. This helps to visually 'anchor' the wall to the ground.

STONE SHELTER
This stone shelter is visually sandwiched between the foreground foothills and the higher peaks in the background.

Suggestion is the key to painting large areas of stone - don't attempt to paint every rock, just focus on a few here and there.

WOODEN HUTS

Wooden huts or shelters are, naturally enough, frequently found in highly-wooded mountainous regions and appeal to artists – painting structures made from natural materials in their own environment.

Wooden huts are best painted by applying an underwash of raw sienna, washed onto dry paper, allowing a few flecks of white paper showing to indicate or suggest the areas where planks are joined. Next, add raw umber to the damp paper, creating a slightly different tone (not all wood planks are the same tone). When this has dried, use a small brush loaded with burnt umber and ultramarine and paint any shadows cast onto the hut. The last application is the 'drawing' of a few selected lines to suggest individual planks of wood.

WOOD GRAIN
The roughness of the wood texture combined with the soft warmth of natural wood tones, creates a study which relies equally on washing paint with a large brush, and 'drawing' with a small brush.

RAW SIENNA

RAW UMBER

BURNT UMBER

ULTRAMARINE

Rather like planks in a complete building, suggest wood grain by employing a few well placed lines of paint 'drawn' with a small brush. The underwash can also be used to show as light areas of grain.

Shadows from wooden structures fall across raised wooden planks and logs, creating an uneven cast. This also necessitates changes in tone, so observe these areas.

It is neither possible nor desirable to paint every single plank whilst sketching wooden huts on site – so choose a few to emphasise, suggesting that the others also exist.

WARM PALETTE
Set amongst the reds, golds and siennas of a flaming forest at the turn of the year, the warmth of the wood in this wooden hut clearly echoed the qualities of the season and was a delight to paint using limited colours.

COOKING STOVE STUDY

Survival in the wilderness involves cooking and eating, and camping gas stoves are ideal for creating a hot meal in cold conditions. They are also good subjects to sketch while waiting for the heat to reach cooking temperature – or, in the case of this particular study, while waiting for the boiled soup to cool a little.

Metal objects, especially curved ones, require some practise as you will need to employ a 'once only' technique – that is, you dampen the paper, pull the paint around the curve of the object with a confident sweeping motion and leave it to dry to a perfectly smooth finish. If you go back to the subject and try to manipulate the paint a little, you will break the surface tension of the drying paint and introduce a brush mark into the otherwise smooth metallic canister.

You may use this technique with cooking pots and pans as well – for best results, any stains or dents should be painted after the initial wash has dried.

The highlights created in the centre (or often to the sides) of canisters can be painted by pulling wet paint into the centre from the left and right, and leaving a very small gap where they join.

SMOOTH SHAPES
The softness of the reflections combined with the symmetry of these curved objects provided a marked contrast with the harsh, sharp, rocky environment, offering a welcome opportunity for gentle tonal mixing.

TORN LETTERING
Sometimes a boost of energy is required through chocolate or glucose bars. The torn lettering here makes an interesting study.

To create a 'real' image of cooking in the wild it is important to illustrate the places where food has boiled over – dampen the paper and apply a mixture of raw and burnt sienna and allow to dry naturally.

The curves on this metallic stove were painted with a mixture of Payne's grey and ultramarine. The paper surface was dampened and the paint pulled from left to right with a small brush and allowed to dry, with a 'puddle' of dark paint forming on the shaded side.

ABOVE THE TIMBERLINE

As you climb higher, above the timberline, the air becomes thinner and clouds frequently obscure your view – often you will be looking down onto clouds forming in the valleys below.

Also, snow and ice will gradually begin to make an appearance in the landscape as it becomes increasingly inhospitable, yet visually appealing.

Looking Down into Valleys

It is a spectacular sight to stand on a high vantage point and look down into the valley below. The most striking aspect is the way in which the peaks of the mountains on the far side of the valley are visually sandwiched between the sky and clouds in the top of the scene, and the mist rising from the valley below, forming thick banks of rolling moisture.

These scenes are probably best painted by starting with the sky and then painting the hills and peaks in the distance – but don't allow the base to dry. Quickly dampen the area of mist or cloud and drop raw sienna towards the top and alizarin crimson and ultramarine mix towards the base. Use as much water as you dare to keep the edges soft and the paint bleeding freely.

Applying wet paint onto damp paper is a very effective technique for creating cloudy areas. Dampen the edge of the cloud and apply the mountain colour to this edge and allow them to bleed.

Cloud Edges

If possible, find an area where you can see above and below the cloud to practise blending and softening the tops and bottoms, sandwiching the 'negative' cloud in the middle.

| RAW SIENNA | ULTRAMARINE | ALIZARIN CRIMSON |

RISING CLOUDS

The early morning period is one of the most magnificent times to paint in mountains and valleys – especially as the light breaks and the colours of the day begin to grow in the clouds as they rise from the deep valleys below your feet.

Clouds hold much colour depending on the atmospheric conditions – with the main colours mixed from raw sienna, ultramarine and alizarin crimson.

LOOKING DOWN ONTO CLOUDS

Looking down onto clouds nestling along the tops of ridges and peaks is an inspiring sight – something that we rarely see unless we are in aircraft.

The key to recording such scenes successfully is to ensure that the cloud appears to roll gently over the top of the peaks in a non-uniform way – clouds are just moisture, which does not sit naturally in a straight line.

First, apply lots of water to the cloud area and drop in a few touches of Payne's grey with a hint of alizarin crimson – this will soon disappear to only a faint, neutral tone. Before this has time to dry, paint the hills and rocks, taking the colour right up to the cloud edge which will soften the paint as the two wet elements meet.

Should the colours blend too quickly, obliterating the white areas around the ridge, blot these areas with a sponge or some kitchen paper to soak up the wet paint. This also dries the paper, preventing any further accidental 'overbleeds'.

SOFT EDGES

A certain degree of haste was required to complete this picture as the rising cloud would soon engulf the entire ridge, leaving nothing of any physical substance left to paint.

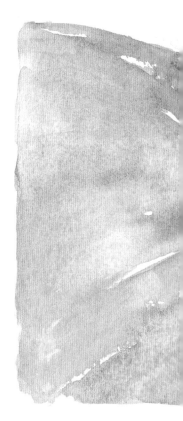

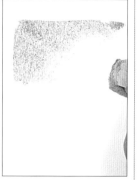

BLOTTING

Kitchen paper can be used to remove wet paint, but this is a much harsher medium and leaves very clear marks, making it more suitable for moving, wispy clouds where definition is required.

SPONGING

Using a sponge to mop up, or remove, watery paint from watercolour paper leaves a soft edge around the sponged area and is suitable for creating soft summer clouds.

If you find that too much paint has run into areas that you wanted to keep light, you can remove the paint by either blotting with kitchen paper, or soaking up the paint with a natural sponge.

Partial blotting around the edges of clouds will help to reveal some soft diluted colour, creating the fleeting effect of low-lying cloud.

Colours in Ice

Some ice that has been created from dirty water will hold a muddy brown colour, otherwise the colours viewed will be largely those reflected from the sky, or those that we as artists choose to apply to suit our particular purpose.

The key to recording ice 'colours' is in the choice of colours used for the shadow mixes. Whilst some colours will impart a sense of cold, others will suggest slightly warmer feelings. Cerulean blue is a fairly cold colour and, when mixed with a very thin, watery alizarin crimson, you will have a shadow paint suitable for freshly frozen ice. However, older ice on slightly less chilly days will benefit from being mixed with Winsor blue, which helps to create a feeling of greater depth and warmth.

To create a soft shadow, apply the paint with a small brush to a previously dampened area of paper. For harder shadows, work directly onto dry paper.

Ice does have a degree of 'thickness' and this can be recorded by painting a hard line of dark violet paint onto dry paper with a small brush.

Ice Tones
Direct sunlight cast onto ice can create 'warm' tones, whilst those areas in direct shade require 'cooler' tones. Try experimenting to see how different you can make any two violet tones.

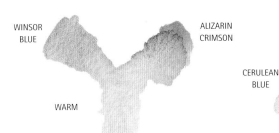

WINSOR BLUE   ALIZARIN CRIMSON

WARM

CERULEAN BLUE   ALIZARIN CRIMSON

COLD

CERULEAN
BLUE

WINSOR
BLUE

ALIZARIN
CRIMSON

The lighter colours reflected from ice are based upon a watery mix of cool blues and violets.

COOL CONTRASTS

Ice bridges can still remain long after the once frozen water has melted, and form an uneasy visual relationship with their immediate environment – but this element of surprise is part of the appeal of painting in hills and mountains.

Rope Study

The higher mountainous regions sometimes require the use of some basic safety equipment – and the bright colours of many of these objects make them ideal subjects for sketchbook studies in the few moments that occur whilst unpacking and checking the working condition of all your backpack contents.

The lighter sections of the rope where the light catches the top are emphasised by darkening the areas directly behind the 'cross over' knots, visually 'pushing' the lighter rope forward.

This particular study relies heavily on the linear qualities of the folded rope and possibly owes more to the initial pencil drawing than any specific watercolour painting technique.

Although the way in which the rope was tied did not create a perfect curve, the method used for painting curved surfaces was still applied.

Using a medium size brush loaded with cadmium orange, pull the paint 'around' the curve of the bulk of the rope – work onto dry paper as this will allow some natural 'highlights' to occur. As the paint dries, apply a shadow colour mixed from ultramarine and alizarin crimson to the shaded areas, working carefully around the overlapping ropes.

The metal karabiners illustrated here are, in fact, not painted at all – the pencil outline drawing indicates the shape, and the snow shadows painted behind them push them out from the white paper.

TEXTURE AND COLOUR
The casual, unposed way in which this climbing rope had been thrown onto the ground gave it a natural look which seemed just right for a sketchbook study.

It is important to be able to follow visually the line of overlapping strands of rope, so be prepared to use the linear qualities of the subject to lead the eye over the top of the curve and out the other side.

SNOW
AND ICE

The sharp blast of ice cold air that welcomes artists brave enough to venture up above the snowline, is indicative of the conditions to come. A world of white, cold greys and the occasional flash of colour await hardy painters – but as always, the rewards are worth any of the discomforts.

ICED-OVER RIVER

Frozen rivers and lakes require very simple treatment – they hold only the colours they reflect from the surrounding hills, woodlands or rocks and crags – and so only require a limited paint range. Most of the colours will be tinged with grey – either made with Payne's grey, ultramarine and umber, or a combination of blues, sienna and crimsons. Use thin washes to exploit the stark quality of the white paper.

FROZEN REFLECTIONS
The bare, skeletal branches of the winter trees provided some fascinating reflections in the frozen river – both positive and negative shapes bouncing from the solid ice.

Painting reflections in ice involves single, one-stroke applications of paint, applied to a dry surface, using horizontal or vertical brushstrokes.

Only 'thin' colours should be used on ice – colours that have been diluted with a lot of water – as they go on easily and dry to a very soft, near translucent tone.

You do not need complex techniques. Use a brushstroke with a 'one stroke' vertical action to pull the paint downwards in clean, clear streaks, leaving flashes of pure white paper in between, reinforcing the 'high key' of the ice.

ICE STUDY
The range of tones in this study was crucial – the more warm and cool tones you use, the more the ice in your picture will 'sparkle'.

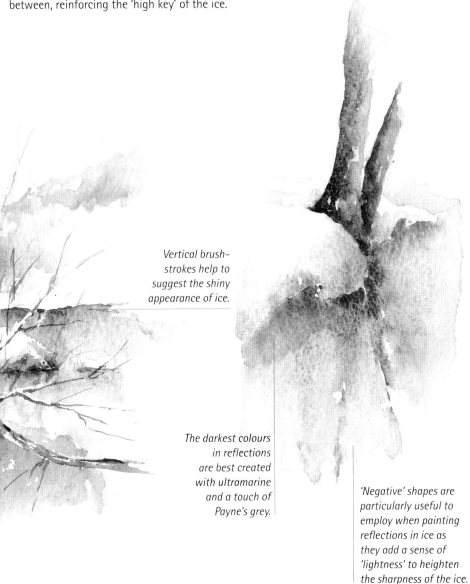

Vertical brush-strokes help to suggest the shiny appearance of ice.

The darkest colours in reflections are best created with ultramarine and a touch of Payne's grey.

'Negative' shapes are particularly useful to employ when painting reflections in ice as they add a sense of 'lightness' to heighten the sharpness of the ice.

SNOW-CAPPED PEAKS

Colours and shadows often become sharper and more intense in the fresher, thinner air of the higher peaks. Whilst the snow is usually pure and freshly fallen, it still needs to be treated to colour in the areas that fall in the shade of the mountain. Strangely, in these extreme atmospheric conditions, it is quite possible to use 'warm' and 'cold' colours within the same composition.

The side of the peak facing the sun can be treated to very gentle toning using a 'warm' mixture of ultramarine and alizarin crimson, reinforcing the fact that the sun is shining on the snow.

The side of the mountain that is in shadow, however, needs to be treated to a 'cold' shadow mixture of Payne's grey and ultramarine – these colours are applied to the snow on the shaded side.

The two warm and cool tones of the shadow colour are blended on the glacier as the two elements join to create the foreground.

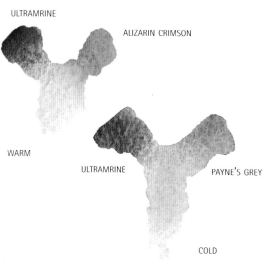

ULTRAMRINE

ALIZARIN CRIMSON

WARM

ULTRAMRINE

PAYNE'S GREY

COLD

DIFFERENT MIXES

Snow visually reflects and absorbs colour – especially the areas in strong shadow. As with ice, experiment to see which tones you can mix to emphasise the differences – 'warm' and 'cold'.

It is important to work onto dry paper, ensuring that much white paper is allowed to 'work' for you, representing the areas of pure, highlighted snow.

The contrast between the dark rocks and the pure unpolluted snow is enhanced by intense dark greys mixed with Payne's grey, ultramarine and burnt umber.

BURNT UMBER

ULTRAMARINE

PAYNE'S GREY

ALIZARIN
CRIMSON

A chisel-headed brush can be particularly useful for recording the sharp, angular glacial ice often found at the base of many high mountains.

DRAMATIC CONTRASTS
The sharpness of the rocks, the harshness of the light and the brilliance of the reflecting snow faces made this high level peak a challenge to paint as many contrasting elements needed to be gently synthesised using only watercolour paints.

Blizzard

Blizzards can occur at any time in the high, snow-clad mountains, but the ferocity of the storm is all part of their visual appeal.

To create the effect of snow, dip an old toothbrush into some masking fluid and flick this onto the paper, creating a random coverage. Masking fluid is a water resistant, rubbery liquid that can be peeled off the paper once paint has been washed over it, leaving flecks of white paper untouched.

Next, flood the sky or cloud area with water and immediately drop burnt umber,

Using Masking Fluid

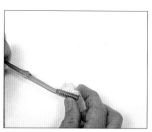

1 First dip an old toothbrush into masking fluid solution, angle the head, and flick the rubbery solution across your paper.

2 When it has dried, gently wash you first coat of paint across the paper – taking care not to dislodge any dried spots of masking fluid. You can now flood the paper with as many colours as you wish, as the paper under the masking fluid is fully protected.

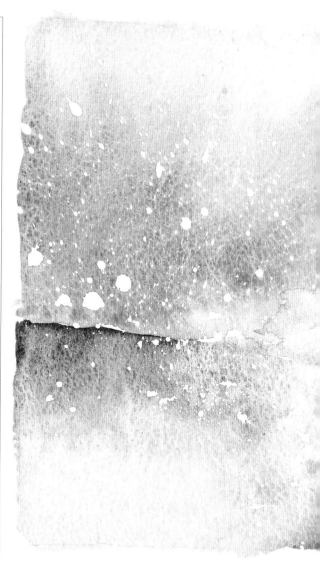

ultramarine, Payne's grey and raw sienna onto the paper – the colours will run and bleed on the surface water, creating a complex set of shapes and tones.

Then, add any appropriate shading to the foreground – this will rarely hold any colour in the middle of a storm – a simple, plain grey will suffice.

When the paper is totally dry, gently rub the surface of the painting to remove the masking fluid, exposing the white paper left untouched by paint.

To create the idea of snow swirling around you, flick masking fluid in a variety of directions, rotating your paper with each 'flick'.

A variety of 'tobacco' colours are often to be seen in storm clouds and are best created by applications of burnt umber, raw sienna and Payne's grey.

It is important to maintain a few flashes of white paper, clearly defining the peaks of the hills.

Snow Storm

When confronted with such an awe-inspiring scene as an approaching snow storm in the mountains, the main area of consideration is to capture an overall impression of the scene through rapid use of colour onto very wet paper – the detail in the foreground becomes surprisingly unimportant.

PRACTISE YOUR SKILLS

The journey through the foothills, mountain passes and high peaks undertaken so far has examined a variety of techniques and colour mixes. Now it is time to examine the techniques involved in completing a full-scale painting, taking you through the processes 'step by step'.

A NATURAL PALETTE

The picture painted for this project relied heavily on some 'natural colours' – raw sienna and burnt umber – both pigments dug from the foothills of the European Alps, as well as the more natural looking olive green. Of course, other colours were used either directly, or as 'mixers', but the overall tone was set by the siennas and umbers. This is something to bear in mind when painting in any outdoor environment – the more 'natural' colours (as opposed to those created by chemists), the more at ease they will look when incorporated in the scene that you are painting.

In the study I made prior to starting this composition, it soon became obvious that the more limited the number of colours used, then the more tones of those colours I would be forced to mix. A box full of colours taken straight from an art store shelf will look very appealing. But what do you do with all those colours other than just use them? This could mean that you will end up using the wrong colours just because you have them. My advice, therefore, is to start off with only a handful of paints and practise mixing as many different tones of these colours as you can.

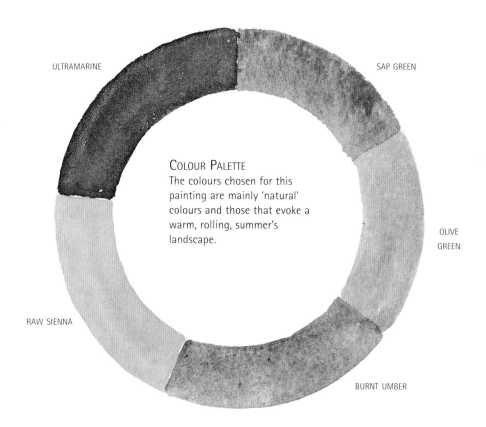

ULTRAMARINE

SAP GREEN

COLOUR PALETTE
The colours chosen for this painting are mainly 'natural' colours and those that evoke a warm, rolling, summer's landscape.

OLIVE GREEN

RAW SIENNA

BURNT UMBER

A raw sienna underwash 'underpins' the olive green, allowing the natural warmth of each colour to work together.

WARM TONES

This study was made quickly, to 'get a feel' for the colours and tones that would be required to undertake a full-scale composition.

ROLLING HILLS

The space between your feet and the horizon is the hardest area to capture effectively in paint. This project examines the use of tones of green tones to suggest distance – the lightest on the far horizon, and the darkest close up in the immediate foreground, with a wide range of tones for the details in between.

Defining the gently rolling hills by the use of shadows is also another feature of this project, again, using tone at all times.

MATERIALS

• 425 gsm (200 lb) watercolour paper

• Brushes – 1 large (size 12), 1 medium (size 8), 1 small (size 2)

• Watercolour pan paints – ultramarine, raw sienna, burnt umber, olive green, sap green

1 The first stage of this painting was to establish the overall mood of the day by painting the sky – this involved dampening the sky area and applying ultramarine to the top using a large brush, letting the paint bleed downwards to create the cloud shapes.

2 While the paper was still damp, I pulled a wash of raw sienna along the base of the cloud shapes and allowed that to bleed upwards into the clouds.

3 *The next stage was to paint a watery wash of raw sienna onto the ground. This was laid onto dry paper, working around the fence to create broken brushstrokes and a few light 'highlight' flashes of white paper.*

4 *Once this underwash had dried, I used pure olive green and, using a small brush, began to paint the hills in the far distance.*

5 *Changing to a medium brush, I continued, starting to define the individual hills with varied tones of olive green and raw sienna.*

6 *Again, this coat of paint was allowed to dry. Sharper definition of the hills was still required, so I introduced some sap green mixed with a little ultramarine and began to paint 'behind' the hills, creating shadows which visually pushed the tops of the hills forward.*

7 *The foreground now had to be brought into sharper focus. I intensified the sap green and ultramarine mixture, dampened the area of paper in the immediate foreground and dropped the paint on – it instantly bled outwards creating a feathery grass blade effect.*

8 *As the foreground wash dried, I ran another line of paint along the base of the tufts of grass with a small brush to create a sense of shading and shadow.*

9 *The rickety old fence could now be painted using a mixture of raw sienna, burnt umber and ultramarine, leaving some flashes of white paper to act as highlights.*

10 *Once the entire fence was completed the whole composition needed to be 'brought together' by the addition of a little sandy colour on the path using raw sienna, and by adding some shadows under the line of the fence.*

DISTANCE

The sense of distance in this gentle landscape has been created by the use of mixtures of green – especially the addition of blue to the hills in the furthest distance. The fence acts as a centre of focus – without this the landscape would still recede away into the distance, but the whole composition would appear very dull without any one specific feature to attract our interest.

The raw sienna underwash can clearly be seen through the thin layer of green paint, adding an element of 'warmth' to the scene.

Shadows underneath the fence visually 'anchor' it to the ground – these were painted with the fence colours mixed with a little green.

MOUNTAIN SCENE

Mountains come in a wide variety of shapes and sizes, and you can never be absolutely certain whether you will be able to see all, or just simply part, of any one at any time. But this level of unpredictability is possibly part of the appeal of painting in the mountain environment.

The coolness of the mist-laden day on which this particular scene was painted required the choice of some 'cold' paints, that is, colours which will impart a sense or feeling of being cold. I used Prussian blue and Payne's grey.

The study made prior to planning out the full-scale painting relied heavily on the use of water-soluble graphite pencil. These are highly portable sketching tools that can be used with or without water, and also help to add to the 'cold' impression by virtue of the greyness of the graphite used in their manufacture. These pencils combine well with watercolour paints when sketching, as they very quickly provide an element of solidity which can take a long time to build up with just watercolour paint, due in part to its natural translucency.

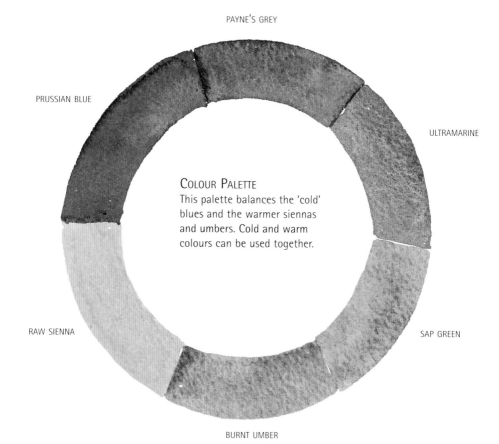

PAYNE'S GREY

PRUSSIAN BLUE

ULTRAMARINE

COLOUR PALETTE
This palette balances the 'cold' blues and the warmer siennas and umbers. Cold and warm colours can be used together.

RAW SIENNA

SAP GREEN

BURNT UMBER

This preliminary study relied on the tonal qualities of water-soluble graphite pencil which would, eventually, have to be translated into 'slate grey' watercolour paints.

ASSESSING THE SCENE

The contrast between the dark rock face and the light mist is one specific area of interest – always look for these contrasts when making sketches.

APPROACHING STORM

It can be truly awe-inspiring, and even frightening, to witness the approach of a storm in mountainous country. The rolling clouds, the darkening sky and the way in which the storm starts to dominate the landscape, are all ominous indicators of trouble ahead. But for those brave enough to stay put and sketch the approaching weather, the rewards are great indeed.

I used a limited palette of colours to link the land and sky, blending wet-into-wet to achieve gradations from light to dark.

MATERIALS
- 500 gsm (250 lb) watercolour paper
- Brushes – 1 large (size 12), 1 medium (size 8), 1 small (size 2)
- Watercolour pan paints – raw sienna, Prussian blue, burnt umber, ultramarine, Payne's grey, sap green
- Water container
- Kitchen paper

1 To establish the rain-laden clouds, I dampened the sky above the mountains. I applied a light wash of raw sienna with the large brush, following the mountain slope. INSET: I applied a dark green mixed from Prussian blue and burnt umber, to dry paper at the top of the sky. I allowed it to blend into the raw sienna. With a damp brush, I moved the paint to create different textures.

2 I added a touch of ultramarine into the green on the right with a damp brush. The colours blend to give dark greys and blues that give form to the underside of the towering storm clouds. Using the large brush, I brought the colour down over the mountain top to suggest the clouds rolling over the ridge.

3 Next, I continued to build the shape of the clouds using a dark mix of Payne's grey, ultramarine and a touch of burnt umber. I dotted this colour with a very damp medium brush on to the clouds and allowed the colour to seep and feather into the green.

4 I varied the intensity of the wash from Step 3 and added it along the top of the sky, tipping the paper to allow the colours to run and blend accidentally. The sky area was now nearly complete and I began to work on the distant hills.

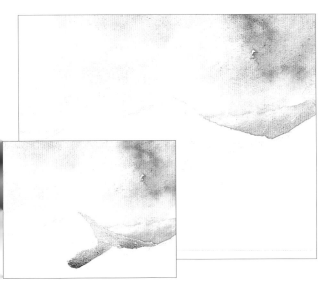

5 I added the distant hills with a cool mix of the sky colour together with a touch of sap green and raw sienna, leaving flashes of white paper to suggest light bouncing off the rocks. I deepened the mix with raw sienna to give a sense of distance and left the paint to form a puddle to give a denser colour. INSET: Using the same blends to vary tones and give depth, I created pockets and shapes of colour with broken strokes to suggest the craggy mountainside.

6 Working with the large brush, I used a darker green-blue mix for the side of the mountain, encouraging the paint to bleed. I added more water to the wash to vary the tone of the mountain in the middle ground, allowing the paint to move freely. I blotted off any excess wash with kitchen paper.

7 At this stage, I assessed the overall painting. The sky and horizon were working well where the different tones and blends had created a feeling of depth and form. The soft edges to the clouds give the impression of approaching weather and blur the division between sky and mountain along the horizon.

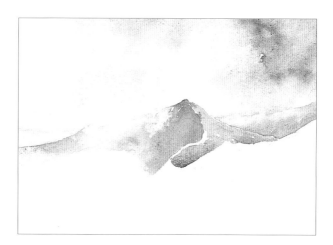

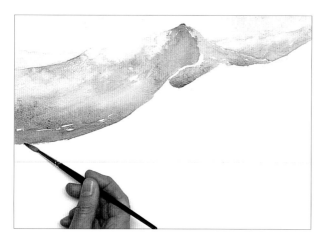

8 I appled a light green to the middle ground with a dry brush. Using a darker mix of ultramarine, burnt umber and a touch of raw sienna, I applied long strokes to follow the sweep of the mountainside. To break the smoothness, I overlaid short strokes of colour leaving a few areas white to represent patches of snow.

9 *Next, I started to work on the foreground. Using a mix of raw sienna and ultramarine, I followed the sweep of the moutainside with the large brush, using rapid brushstrokes and grading the tones from light to dark to give a sense of recession. While the paint was still damp, I used the medium brush to reinforce the detail of the underside of the rock outcrops.*

10 *I used a small brush with touches of the darker mix from Step 9 to drop paint and water onto the hillside to break the broad bands of colour, leaving the paint to feather and blend freely. INSET: I added more intense colour to the foreground area, using a damp brush to blend the colours and give the effect of dappled light.*

11 *In the final stage, I allowed the paint to dry slightly, then reworked some areas layering wet paint to follow the pattern of the dry paint beneath to give the impression of pockets of mist. Using a small brush, I ran a dark brown mix of ultramarine and dark umber into the paint.*

GRADED TONE

The limited palette used in this painting has been extended to achieve a remarkable range of tones for both the sky and the mountainside. The progression from light to dark across the mountainside gives the impression of a vast landscape. The layering of colours in the sky has resulted in a subtle suggestion of towering rain clouds rolling across the mountain tops.

The varied tones give the suggestion of light coming through the clouds.

The light wash brought over the moutain ridge suggests rolling clouds of mist.

*I knocked back the harsh
white of the ridge with a
light wash of sap green
with a touch of raw sienna.*

ROCK AND BOULDER PATH

Whilst the actual path only takes up a very thin part of this composition in terms of space used, it is in fact central to the success of the whole picture as it provides a means of visual access to the mountains in the distance. Our eyes are naturally drawn to such linear facets rather than the flatter areas of mountain meadow surrounding the path and this, as a consequence, provides the area of central interest or focus within the picture frame.

It was, therefore, important not to get carried away with the actual number of boulders or stones that were present in the path as this could make it dominate the scene if it contained too much detail. A simple suggestion of their shapes, therefore, suddenly became very important.

As in the study of rocks and boulders, it is not really possible or desirable to include every pebble, rock, stone or chip that you see. Instead, focus on a few prominent rocks or stones – these need not necessarily be the largest, in fact a spread of sizes is particularly desirable. The most effective method of suggesting such objects is spacing – make sure that you space your 'drawn' rocks unevenly without any discernible pattern. This makes them all the more interesting to look at.

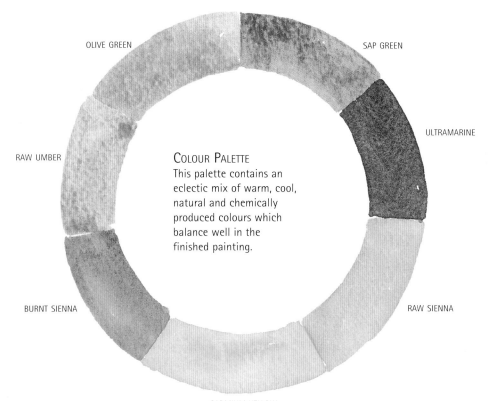

OLIVE GREEN

SAP GREEN

ULTRAMARINE

RAW UMBER

COLOUR PALETTE
This palette contains an eclectic mix of warm, cool, natural and chemically produced colours which balance well in the finished painting.

RAW SIENNA

BURNT SIENNA

CADMIUM YELLOW

SPACES IN BETWEEN

'Negative' shapes can make even more interesting shapes than the 'positive' rocks and boulders.

A watery underwash onto dry paper will dry unevenly leaving watermarks which can be turned into rocks and boulders by making a few appropriate marks around them.

The negative shapes of the shadowed cracks and fissures help to define the pattern of the solid rocks and boulders that make up the path.

ROCKY PATH

This project involved following the sweeping line of a rocky path through lush green lowlands to mountains rising in the far distance.

The path was the centre of focus throughout the painting process and needed special attention towards the end – exactly how much detail to paint in and just how much to suggest was the key question.

MATERIALS
- 425 gsm (200 lb) watercolour paper
- Brushes – 1 large (size 12), 1 medium (size 8), 1 small (size 2)
- Watercolour pan paints – sap green, ultramarine, Payne's grey, raw sienna, olive green, cadmium yellow, burnt sienna, burnt umber, raw umber

1 *The scene was sketched out including some of the details on the path and then a wash of ultramarine was applied to the sky.*

2 *Then, to establish the basic colour for the distant mountains, working onto damp paper, sap green, ultramarine and Payne's grey were painted at the base. The damp paper encouraged the colours to merge to create a mist around the peak. As this dried, a wash of raw sienna was applied to the mountain meadows, working onto dry paper with a dry brush.*

3 Once this had dried a medium size brush was used to drag a wash of olive green and raw sienna across the meadows, leaving flashes of the underwash showing through.

4 The row of trees on the right could now be established. The season required the use of autumnal colours – raw sienna, burnt sienna, cadmium yellow and some sap green. These colours were painted onto dry paper to create shapes in the trees.

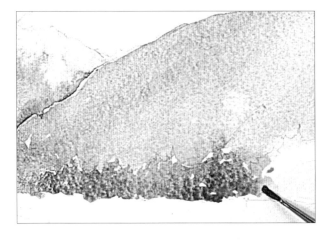

5 To make them stand out in the landscape, a small brush was used to paint a very dark mix of sap green and ultramarine along the bottom of the trees, creating shaded areas and 'anchoring' them to the ground.

6 Next, I started to work on the immediate foreground. Once again, I applied a wash of the warm raw sienna with a large brush, working onto dry paper to achieve a patchy appearance.

7 While the underwash was drying, I mixed some raw sienna with sap green and a touch of burnt umber to give the colour a little more visual 'weight'. Starting at the bottom of the paper, I pulled the paint upwards towards the horizon, allowing the underwash to break through in parts.

8 It was now time to look closely at the path. I had sketched a few of the boulders already and intended to use paint to suggest others. A raw umber wash was dragged along the length of the path using broken brushstrokes.

9 As this was drying, I mixed a combination of raw umber, burnt umber and Payne's grey and, using a small brush, began to pick out a few areas of dark and shade. The paint bled on the damp paper and dried with a watermark.

10 The final stage of this painting was to use a small brush to 'draw' some of the rocks and boulders in the immediate foreground.

SUBTLE DETAILS

Suggestion, rather than excessive detail, was the key to this painting. Shadows and shading are suggested on the row of trees in the middle ground. The rocks and boulders in the foreground are not all painted as positive shapes – many are the result of negative shapes that have occurred as watery paint has dried onto a dry paper surface.

The misty effect on top of the mountain was created by allowing the colours applied to the rock face at the bottom to bleed upwards into damp paper with no other intervention.

The raw sienna underwash can be seen through the broken brush marks, acting as highlights on an otherwise flat surface.

SNOW-COVERED PEAKS

One of the main problems with painting snow is exactly how do you paint white snow onto white watercolour paper. The answer is two-fold. First, much of the snow will paint itself – pure, untouched white watercolour paper will produce the sharpest, clearest white you will find which certainly is the equal of the glare given off by most snow fields. Second, many areas of snow will not actually look white as they will be in the shadow of overhanging ledges, rocks, or even large boulders. These areas need to be painted with a mixture of soft blues and violets. These natural blue-grey tones are clearly reflected in my choice of colours for this particular project: one warm blue (ultramarine), one cool blue (cerulean) and Payne's grey, which is a chemically-manufactured paint using a combination of blue and black.

Personally, I never use pure black in watercolour paintings as it has the effect of visually 'flattening' anything that it comes into contact with. To create a really dark tone that will do a similar job, I recommend a strong mixture of burnt umber and ultramarine – the resulting colour is rich with a much better visual depth.

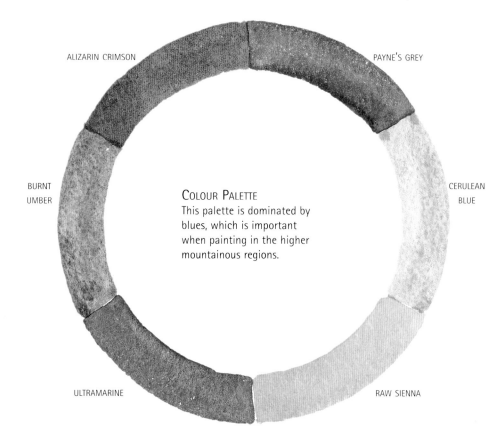

ALIZARIN CRIMSON

PAYNE'S GREY

BURNT UMBER

CERULEAN BLUE

COLOUR PALETTE
This palette is dominated by blues, which is important when painting in the higher mountainous regions.

ULTRAMARINE

RAW SIENNA

Use as many tonal mixtures of blues and violets as you can possibly mix to achieve a sense of depth and recession when painting snow.

SNOW FLURRY

Snow is frequently caught by the wind and blown in all directions. Always flick masking fluid from more than one position to suggest this movement.

FALLEN SNOW

This particular painting relied heavily on the interplay of light between the sky and the snow-clad mountainside – both served to reflect each other.

As snow holds no real colour of its own, it is our job as artists to look for the colours that are reflected and to turn those into the correct mixture of paints.

This project also relied heavily on the use of pure white – the purity of the paper being preferable to any white paint.

MATERIALS
- 425 gsm (200 lb) watercolour paper
- Brushes – 1 large (size 12), 1 medium (size 8), 1 small (size 2)
- Watercolour pan paints - cerulean blue, ultramarine, alizarin crimson, raw sienna, burnt umber, Payne's grey

1 The sky was dampened and a wash of cerulean blue was run along the mountain tops and pulled upwards. Before this could dry, a wash of ultramarine was run along the top of the paper and pulled downwards, creating a graduated wash.

2 While the paper and surface paint were still damp, I introduced a soft violet colour into the sky, mixed from ultramarine and alizarin crimson, washing it down from the top with a large brush.

3 The soft violet used in the sky was also used to 'block in' the main areas of shadow on the mountainside, working with a medium size brush onto dry paper.

4 The rock underneath the snow line was painted next, using a small brush with a mixture of raw sienna and Payne's grey. I pulled the paint upwards to meet the snow where it was left to dry with a hard line.

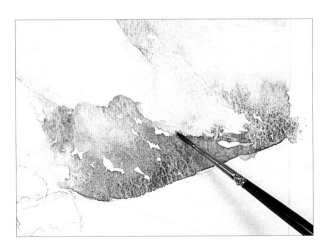

5 I then mixed a stronger version of the soft violet by increasing the amount of ultramarine, and began to reinforce the darkest shaded sections by painting them with a small brush.

6 Having established the very light tones of shadows and the deepest, darkest areas of shade, I was able to judge exactly how light or dark the 'middle' tones should be. These were mixed with a little raw sienna and the original soft violet, and painted onto outcrops across the mountain.

7 It was now time to concentrate on the immediate foreground by painting in the shadows cast by the dips and protrusions in the snowfield, highlighting the stone cairn as a negative shape.

8 The cairn was then painted with a raw sienna underwash, working onto dry paper with broken brushstrokes. A little Payne's grey was applied to the right-hand side as it dried to begin to suggest light and shade.

9 *When this had dried, the cracks between the boulders and the shadows were 'drawn' using a small brush and a mixture of raw sienna, burnt umber and Payne's grey.*

10 *The final stage was to strengthen the shadow cast by the cairn using the dark violet mix from Step 5. This was painted onto dry paper at first, but the edges were 'washed out' using clean water to soften the final appearance.*

Snow Colours

The variety of tones of violet in the sky, the snow and on the shading on the rocky outcrops proved to be a major feature of this painting – sometimes applied to dry paper and left to dry with a hard line, and at other times washed onto damp paper to provide a softer edge. Even the pile of stone cairns in the immediate foreground contained an element of violet – reflected from both the sky and the surrounding snow.

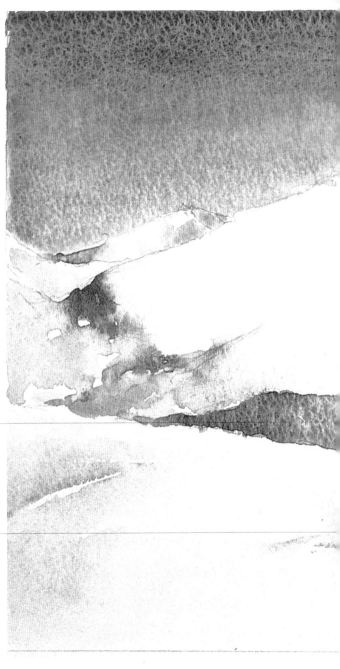

Darker blues and violets are used to give the impression of deep, cold shadows and to draw areas of snow into the visual foreground.

Soft blues and violets are used to create the illusion of distance over large areas – especially in mountainous regions.

INDEX